CATHERINE RUSSO EPSTEIN

Walk with Power, Peace, Presence and Purpose

YOUR GUIDE TO STOP LIVING ON AUTOPILOT
AND START LIVING A SOUL ALIGNED LIFE

TABLE OF CONTENTS

FOREWORD

Did you forget something?

Did you forget that you are a radiant, cosmic being who is here (on this Earth) for a temporary ride- to learn, to grow and to know- and to follow your soul path?

Oh, I know it's tough to truly remember that; given that we have jobs, spouses, families, elders and younger ones, traffic, homes and other details of human existence.

But, I'm curious.

Do you live so lightly that you are just floating on the top of life, not really living to the breadth and depth of it all? Surface skimming if you will- just running through the motions of having a life; yet not really LIVING?

A dear friend just told me that her husband got her attention by saying this to her: He mentioned that she's always working, or running around helping others, and when she's home, she's always tired. You know what her reaction was? (Honestly, I thought she was going to lose her shit on him and tell

him to pull his weight more, or just flip out on him)
But she didn't. She realized he was right- so she
made a commitment to herself, right then and there -
to **S L O W** down.

And I think she will- up to the point where the cycle
begins all over again.

Have you had this happen to you?

You wake up in the morning with grand plans for the
day- but just after the coffee, your phone buzzes with
other people needing your energy and attention.

Barely time to eat right, you've spent the day helping
others, taking care of all the things, work things,
family things, friend things… no time to yourself- and
before you know it- you numb out in front of the TV
and fall asleep…

You wish you could just go away for a week (or two)
and find some inner peace- but that never seems to
happen.

If that scenario sounds a bit familiar, keep reading.

See, the challenge in this life is to actually rise above
the mind-numbing behaviors of auto-pilot and begin
to consciously create our lives.

Not in a "sell everything and go live in the woods"

kind of way- but a strategic, mindful, creative, thoughtful way of living.

Let me explain.

Our role here on Earth is to expand and to grow. Stagnation is the antithesis of our nature. The universe is always expanding, (ever watch a flower bloom through a crack in the sidewalk?)

Even though the goal is to expand and grow, everything (including us) has its cycles. Inhale and Exhale, Ebb and Flow, Expansion and Contraction. We just need to know our place in the cycle and how to manage through it.

I've created this book for you- to help you master your energy and to step into (embody) the TRUE radiant you. Don't worry if it all sounds too woo-woo, fantasy, or sci-fi. It's possible, it's easy AND I will show you how.

Keep your mind open and read on.

There is no doubt that we are living in powerful times- and it is our choice to be fully immersed in the energy that the Universe is offering.

We are at a critical time in humanity's evolution.

If you're reading this, I know you can feel it -
Everyone is in transition!

While this transition looks different for everyone, the universe is doing its job to wake us and shake us!

If you're ready to stand in your power and create a soul aligned life, this guide is for you!

Get ready and learn how to walk with *Power, Peace, Presence and Purpose*

INTRODUCTION

--------------- + ✦ ✦ ✦ ✦ + --------------

"To Marry one's Soul - Being true to who we are means carrying our Spirit in the center of our darkness."

~ Mark Nepo

There lies within each and every one of us an essence, a great storehouse of power beyond what our mere mortal mind can grasp. You can't see it, but once you can fully trust that it is there- you become unstoppable. Learning to step out beyond your immediate surroundings and circumstances- is the great challenge before you.

Sometimes, we get this gnawing urge to change up our lives. We might wish things were different, in big or small ways, but sometimes we get overwhelmed. That overwhelm can lead to inertia. And, that's when we say that we're feeling "stuck."

My goal in writing this book is to help you to:

(1)

Remember that inner essence is always there

(2)

Help you to access it

(3)

Teach you to direct and harness the energy toward your dreams and desires

Once you know that you can access this inner essence and how to do it easily, you can indeed walk with ***Power, Peace, Presence and Purpose.***

I understand the challenge for many is that we simply get too caught up in our "little" lives- and are so busy putting out the fires of the day, that we get bogged down in the relentless pursuit of "success."

As a Transformational Life Coach who has helped thousands of souls to live more heart centered lives. I've seen the gamut of what I call "living on autopilot." I define it as "The mere act of existing in this life, and not living the true depth of the full human experience." We have been taught that emotions are icky, so we have developed many coping skills to help us avoid feeling too much. I've seen people spend more time and energy into the latest Netflix series than they do with their immediate relationships. Don't get me wrong, there's nothing like relaxing in front of the TV at night; but where do we draw the line when it interferes with our ability to relate to others?

In other words- how can we live the FULL range of the human experience (embracing the plethora of emotions) while staying connected to our families, friends, co-workers and communities?

Indeed, the world has gotten a whole lot smaller (since the internet); but has it brought us closer?

I will touch on one more thing. Although the world does seem like it's falling apart, but in reality, it's the breaking apart of things that are not sustainable. Many of the systems that have been put into place were based on the old, patriarchal, greed-based paradigm.

That's what's ending.

It really is UP TO US, to bring forth the new – one human being at a time.

One of the most important things we can learn to do is to gain mastery over our thoughts, feelings and emotions- so we can consciously create better lives.

While it seems to be an overly simplistic view - *"just gain mastery over yourself and the rest will fall into place."* It really isn't simplistic, nor is it easy.

We've been indoctrinated and sold a bill of goods of what a successful life looks like, and in my humble opinion; that is NOT why we were put on this Earth at this time.

It is our function to bring higher consciousness and awareness to raise the vibe of all humanity- to bring about the shift of the ages that have been talked about for millennia. And no, it's not the New Age bullshit that taught us to "light and love" and spiritually bypass our shadow and darker nature.

What I hope to impart in this book, is to help remind you to tap into your True Self, your energy and live out the Divine Blueprint for your life. My goal is to help you take the lead and commit to adding to the betterment of this world.

By doing this, you can help to make an impact, leave a legacy and help to guide humanity into the next phase.

Are you up to the challenge?

POWER

"When our behaviors match our intentions, when our actions are equal to our thoughts, when our minds and our bodies are working together...there is an immense power behind any individual."

~ Joe Dispenza

I n this chapter, we are going to talk about *Power*. What it is, how to access it, how to manage it and how to master it.

In a moment, I will talk about the 3 kinds of power; *Inner Power, Outer Power and Higher Power.*

But let's start with the broader view first.
Let me ask you how you feel about Power.

Do you stand fully in your energy or are you leaking energy in certain situations or with certain people?

Your power is your life force, your energy, your connection to Source- it is the totality of your Being.

Let's be clear about one thing. Power is NOT about wielding control over another using fear or manipulative tactics- (that's a toxic trait that has dominated society for eons).

When I talk about POWER, I use it in the sense that you are connected to your energy, your inner being and your heart and mind ALL together. It is from this perspective that involves the 3 kinds of power.

For the purposes of this book and my teachings, I talk about 3 kinds of Power.

They are:

Inner Power, Outer Power and Higher Power.

Let's break it down:

(1)

Inner Power is our connection to our emotional state, our sense of self and how we project ourselves out into the world.

(2)

Outer Power is our mastery of our energy field- how we are strong or weak in how we relate to others. We know when we are leaking energy, or absorbing too much.

(3)

Higher Power is our connection to the flow of the Divine essence within us. It is also about recognizing the Divine in everything.

When these three are all in harmony with each other, we emanate a sense of self-mastery.

True story:

When I was younger, I was a people pleaser. I stayed quiet in most situations, and I did not speak my truth. Although I wanted to be bold and daring, I constantly gave away my power- to keep the peace.

Even as a young adult, navigating my way through the corporate world and new relationships, I found myself firmly entrenched in old patterns.

"keep quiet, don't make waves, lay low, operate under the radar"

I thought these behaviors kept me safe, but in reality, only served to tamp down my authentic voice and not live to my full potential.

I realized that these were safety mechanisms put in place at a very early age.

But, as author Barbara Stanny (now Huson) said,

"the coping skills that served you as a child, will suffocate you as an adult."

She's so right about that!

Fast forward to now: As a human, it took a lot of courage and soul-work for me to leave an unhealthy marriage. And, as a spiritual seeker; and empowerment coach for many years, I have done massive amounts of work on myself.

The "work" still continues.

My favorite quote:

"I AM a work in progress, as long as I work on myself, I will progress."

One question:

Are you living life on your own terms? As you ponder the answer, think about what "on your own terms" means to you.

We all want to feel in control of our own destiny, but how many of us feel stuck in the rut of same-old-same old? Are you ready to reclaim your power and to enjoy Living Life on your own terms?

In my own life and in the lives of people I work with; it is sometimes hard to get out of the cycle of complacency. You get comfortable and maybe you feel a stirring of discontent, but it isn't really enough to stand up and shake it off. You may feel a bit off kilter, but can you identify its source? You are living each day by tending to the tasks of surviving, but are you really living? Take a moment to sit with those questions and then listen to your answers.

Transformation doesn't have to be the "hit by the cosmic 2×4" kind of change. We've all had that at some point, and it can be quite an upheaval. We've all heard the nudges and whispers of the inner self and we've ignored it or made excuses. Then, WHAM, we get whacked by the "cosmic 2 x 4" to force change upon us. The good news is that it doesn't have to be so dramatic. Sometimes it is just one small step that can move us in the right direction. Doesn't that sound more palatable than change being forced up on us?

Since I like to keep things simple…. (breathe in)…..and easy…(breath out)….the first place to start is with a renewed commitment to getting back in control and to lead a more Heart Centered life.
If you've taken a more resigned approach and think that you can't make the changes you want, think again.

Here are some steps that show you how to move from feeling Power-less to feeling Powerful! I share these steps with my clients, and I use them in my own life!

✦ Commitment ✦

Start with this moment to re-new your commitment to your life and your journey. When you accept where you are right now, it helps to bring your awareness back into the present. Accept the feeling/emotion that is up for you and check in with your body. From this point, you can take stock of what is in your life, thus identify what can stay and what needs to go. It is in the accepting and not resisting that can help take you to the next step. Give yourself permission to change.

✦ Clarity ✦

The next step is to get very clear on where you want to go. What is it that you want? Sit down with your journal and make a list of 10 or more words/ qualities that make you feel alive again. (examples: Compassionate, Peaceful, Joyful, Bold, Caring, Present, Energetic, Courageous) you get the idea. Once you've identified the top 10, narrow your list to the three that speak to your soul the most. Don't "think" about the right answer, but allow what is in your heart at this moment. View the situation from a higher perspective, so you can regain the feeling of being empowered. Feel all of your energy returning back to your core. This must happen before you can focus on what to do next. Once you've identified your 3 words, set your intention to embody these traits and write them on an index card. Although these words change often for me, my over-riding one reads *'Awake, Aware, and Alive.'* What are your words?

✦ Connection ✦

This is the step where you have reconnected with your highest and best self. Now the vision for your life can begin to unfold. This is the 3rd step, but by no means the final one. After you've pulled in all of your energy, you are now ready to listen more fully to the inner callings of your soul. No more excuses, or denials- just a firm commitment to re-gain your POWER. After you've made the connection, just ask for guidance for the next step. Trust that it will unfold for you, then follow the stirrings of your heart.

Once you RE-Commit to yourself, Re-Clarify your vision, and Reconnect to your best self to regain your POWER, you will send a message to the Universe that you are ready. Taking these steps will help you to live life on your own terms!

Our "human" experience is always leading us to expansion, understanding and awareness.... even through all the tough lessons.

When we can come to the realization that we are spiritual beings having a spiritual experience, in a human body, we can more easily control our own reactions to circumstances in the outer world.

In other words, the only thing we can control is our reactions to these external forces that are beyond our control. Staying tapped into the power within will help you through.

In this world of outer distractions, where there is so much vying for our attention; it's important to keep being mindful of our energy.

Boundaries - Another part of standing in your Power is understanding your own energy leaks. Otherwise known as boundaries. As I've come to know- boundaries are all about teaching other people how to treat us. This can come from a long period of tolerating unhealthy behavior until we've had enough. Or, as I like to call it, "the line in the sand." Having healthy boundaries is all about our relationship with ourselves; and making that clear with others.

This is what I mean about accessing, connecting and standing in your *Power.*

REMEMBER:

Nothing outside of you has power over you unless you allow it.

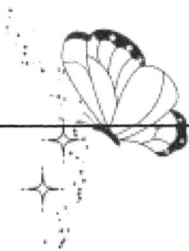

Chapter Summary:

There are three kinds of power. Inner, Outer and Higher- 1) <u>Inner Power</u> is our connection to our emotional state, our sense of self and how we project ourselves out into the world. 2) <u>Outer Power</u> is our mastery of our energy field- how we are strong or weak in how we relate to others. 3) <u>Higher Power</u> is our connection to the flow of the Divine essence within us. When these three are all in harmony with each other, we emanate a sense of self-mastery.

Exercise:

Take a few minutes each day and connect with your energy. Practice becoming aware of the 3 kinds of power and learn when you are out of balance or when your energy is running smoothly.

PEACE

+ ✦ ✦ ✦ +

"Never be in a hurry; do everything quietly and in a calm spirit. Do not lose your inner peace for anything whatsoever, even if your whole world seems upset."

~ Saint Francis de Sales

Here's a bold statement.

N othing is as Important as your Inner Peace.

What that means is to not let anything outside of you affect your inner state. That's a tall order given that we live in a pretty hectic society- but that is what our true practice is.

It's about accepting the upheavals, dealing with emotions, and facing the certain ups and downs that are all part of living the human experience. But, let me be clear; this acceptance of what is, is NOT about giving in or letting people take advantage of us. Nor is about letting abusive behavior continue on any level.

PEACE is more a radical state of living inside our true nature as much of the time as we can- so that WHEN the cosmic 2x4 hits; we can deal with the situation all the while staying tapped into that inner state.

This requires practice. Sometimes, our response is a knee-jerk reaction that blurts out before we have time to process.

One thing I've learned along this journey, is to not look for PEACE outside of yourself. Depending on where you look, there's always chaos and there's always PEACE...

The good news is, you get to decide what you are focusing on. When you focus on what is good and true- that's what you'll see.

Stay Peaceful, Stay Positive...

I wrote this back in 2008 and it still rings true today:

"Peace within is peace without. Peace is a state of mind and being. When you are centered and peaceful, it radiates out from your heart center to those around you. No matter what frenzy is going on, you will have the ability to stay rooted ~this is what we strive for. No matter how challenging the situation is, we stay focused and steady. The place of peace is available to those who are ready to tap into it. We only need to remember...The seeds of peace have been planted by the Divine...it is up to us to sow them."

Picture peace pulsating throughout the planet. Picture peace pulsating throughout your heart. Is it possible? We need to remember that for every positive thought, a lot of negativity gets canceled out. If you believe that the seeds of peace are already planted, and are only waiting for us to sow them- then peace is possible. Transmitting a peaceful vibe begins within our own hearts.

A big part of our "work" is to maintain the connection to our inner peace no matter what is happening in the outside world. This is not to say that we must stay in unhealthy or toxic or unsafe situations- far from it. It is about loving ourselves enough to break free of anything that is draining or challenging to our psyche. If you find yourself in that situation, begin NOW to gather the resources and support to get out.

When you make it your job to walk with PEACE through life, you'll notice a certain calmness you hadn't felt before.

"Make Peace with Where you are" I "heard" these words while driving one day.

And, as I allowed the words to settle through me, I realized that when you incorporate this truth- all struggles will cease. Yes, they will cease. No matter what curveballs will be thrown your way, no matter who acts in a way you don't like, no matter what the outside world looks like, you can ride through the storm of life when you are at peace with where you are in this moment.

Wouldn't it be wonderful to live in a way where you are at peace with what is- all the time? "Keep your eye on the prize"- means to indeed stay focused on your ultimate goal- and that is to live in a world filled with peace and harmony. The only requirement is to stay in touch with your thoughts and feelings throughout your day. The task is indeed to be mindful of the flow of how you are feeling- and this will be your guide. Check in with your inner self, and realign where necessary.

The following is a metaphor that came to me recently: While so many of us have been slogging our way through healing, lessons and muck- you may have had the feeling that you are revisiting many lessons you thought you had learned. What was shown to me in a vision was that we are indeed continuing to dig deep and deal with remnants of that which we thought we had already dealt with. The vision was this: imagine you are using tweezers to pluck out splinters. These shards and splinters are that which is left of what no longer serves. Yes, many have done the critical work and released most of the energies of old patterning. Think about these splinters as the further vestiges of the major clearing that so many of us have been through.

There are two schools of thought about this- and to me, it all boils down to a very simplistic viewpoint.

To "make peace with where you are"
implies non attachment to
what is going on around you.

It speaks to releasing any forms of control or resistance. When you do this, it places the responsibility for your peace and happiness directly with you. You are not dependent upon the outside forces for your joy. You are in full control of how you choose to react or not react to any person or situation. This is for you to decide- and when you wake up every morning, you get to choose how you will feel throughout the day. There will always be stuff going on in your outer world, and the world at large.

This is not to imply passivity or hiding one's head in the sand. Those days are over and we can clearly see that anything that has been built upon greed or envy is quickly and rapidly deteriorating. Anything in our own lives that was created from an unconscious thought process (such as denial)- is also up in our faces for re-negotiation. But now, we know what we wish to create in our own lives and in the world- we can take the steps necessary to bring out a loving and peaceful world. We can involve ourselves in organizations that bring together the common cause, whether it be to help the hungry, eradicate disease, help animals or the environment in whatever way empowers us.

We are also empowered when we cease complaining about the state of the world and live our own truth.

Stand fully, own your power and direct your thoughts toward a more positive and loving existence. Don't fight the way things are, that is not the energy you wish to put forth. Instead, be peaceful with the NOW moment knowing that you may take steps toward living the better life you wish to create. Let go of the struggles of blame, and other lower thought forms. Allow this moment to be- *as perfection*….

As we know and have heard many times, we won't find peace if we are looking outside of ourselves. We won't find it in our external world and the behavior of others. We only have to look within- and connect with that very still part of ourselves. It lies within the depths of our heart. **You own peace, you have peace, you are peace!**

Continue to radiate joy in your life and to *"make peace with where you are."*
Remember to take your peace with you!

REMEMBER:

Let nothing disrupt your inner peace.

Peace is our natural state of being- and it's important to remember that we can keep choosing peace over and over. With the state of the world these days it's even more crucial to stay tapped into the peace. When things knock us sideways (and they will), we can choose to come back to our peaceful center over and over again.

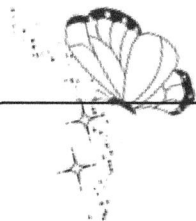

Chapter Summary:

How do we make sense of the external world? By staying tapped into our inner self, our inner being- the part of us that is one with the universe.
As often as you can, throughout the day- become aware of your inner being- your center, your core. Keep returning to the place within and radiate peace from there.

That's how we impact the world.

Exercise:

Begin by putting yourself in a comfortable seated position. After becoming centered and grounded, imagine that a beam of light is streaming out of the top of your head- all the way up to the angelic realm.

Become more relaxed as you feel the transmission of peace pouring down through you- and send your love and gratitude back to the Angels. Tap into the loving vibe emanating and let it fill your body. Just feel it flowing out and around you- send it out in waves to your loved ones, your community, your country and the world! Picture peace pulsating throughout the planet.

"Everything we do is infused with the energy with which we do it. If we're frantic, life will be frantic. If we're peaceful, life will be peaceful. And so, our goal in any situation becomes inner peace."

~ Marianne Williamson

PRESENCE

------------- ✦ ✦ ✦ ✦ ✦ -------------

"The mind can go in a thousand directions, but on this beautiful path, I walk in peace. With each step, the wind blows. With each step, a flower blooms."

-Thich Nhat Hanh

H ave you ever had a conversation with someone and you just knew they were "checked out?" They went through the motions, nodding, "uh-uh," in all the right places- but you just knew they weren't all there.

Conversely, have you had a conversation with someone who made eye contact, was fully engaged in what you were saying, they asked insightful questions and you felt they were genuinely invested in the conversation. When you looked back on the conversation, you noticed that they were PRESENT.

See the difference? Admittedly, I've been both and

the first one isn't so pleasant- it makes us feel we're not worth talking to, or even worse; just taking up space. The second has a way of bringing us to life, feeding off the energy and making us want to be present to the other as well.

The other cool thing about PRESENCE is that there doesn't need to be any words exchanged. You just FEEL it when a person enters a room, when a person is on stage, or even a salesperson in a store.

But I'm going to go even deeper- it's not just about "charisma" or personality- it's all about ENERGY. Energy doesn't lie.

What does it truly mean to be PRESENT? According to Eckhardt Tolle; *"Presence is a state of being that is always accessible to us. We reach a state of presence (become fully present) by tapping into our inner awareness (beyond ego) to become fully conscious of the present moment."*

In my own definition, I equate Presence with Mindfulness. Although not exactly the same- for our purposes they can be overlapped. Truthfully, you really can't be PRESENT without being Mindful or vice versa.

The other part of Presence is Mindfulness- my definition: *"Awareness of the present moment without judgment."*

When we are present, we are in the moment- and **aware of our thoughts, feelings and emotions-** yet we are just witnessing these and not judging.

That is certainly a challenge for most of us- to be PRESENT during tough times and situations.

Let's go even deeper.
Being PRESENT during the "storms" of our life is akin to being in the eye of the hurricane. Chaos is swirling all around, but in that little sweet spot, we are safe, dry and untouched.

Yet there's still more.

Being PRESENT to what we are feeling IN THE MOMENT- is acknowledging the feeling (as uncomfortable as it may be)- and just allowing it to be.

When we are PRESENT in life, we get to be in the full experience! The energy, the flow, the radiance, the nuances, the little things. From here we make more conscious choices because we are in tune with ourselves.

We get to BE the radiant beings that we ARE!

What are some other ways we can be PRESENT?

- ✓ by speaking up when things are not right
- ✓ by pulling our energy from situations or people
- ✓ by listening to our bodies
- ✓ by naming the feeling
- ✓ by saying "NO"
- ✓ by trusting ourselves
- ✓ by honoring our own needs
- ✓ by making choices out of LOVE (not fear)
- ✓ by fully accepting ourselves
- ✓ by practicing radical self-care

Practice Presence: Bring your awareness to the present moment, stop worrying about the past or obsessing about the future.

REMEMBER:

Bring your awareness to the here and now. Presence is a way of Being.

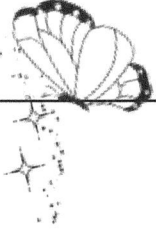

Chapter Summary:

PRESENCE is a state of being, a conscious awareness of being in the present moment. It takes practice to be present to ourselves and others- it's the opposite of living on autopilot. When we are present, we're not thinking about the past or worrying about the future- we are in the timeless NOW.

Exercise:

Set a timer for 5 minutes. Sit quietly for a moment and let yourself be present. Observe the sounds around you, observe your thoughts, feelings and emotions. Pay attention to whatever comes up (even if it's uncomfortable). It's very important to observe without judgment.

PURPOSE

------------- ✦ ✦ ✦ ✦ ✦ -------------

"Everyone has a unique part to play in the healing of the world"

~ Marianne Williamson

C an you imagine rediscovering your gifts, talents, and passions, and using them as the foundation for the life of your dreams?

You're at a crossroads, either externally or internally, and you want to infuse your life with purpose.
Only, you …

Aren't even sure what your purpose is, much less how to live it.

Purpose is a nebulous word- it's been bandied about and the meaning has been diluted for the sake of having a new "buzzword."

But, let's break it down.

Our purpose in life is much more than our achievements, our progeny, our material gains, our bank accounts.

As one new age guru said, "we weren't just born to work until we die" or something like that.

Recently I was in an office building and as I crossed the lobby to head to my destination, I noticed with sadness a certain air of resignation. People were heading to the cafeteria, their office or the restroom; while looking down at their phones, deep in whatever was on their screen. Occasionally they would look up so they didn't bump into someone- they reminded me of automatons immersed in their programmed tasks. Even more interesting, was when I would catch someone's eye; I would smile- connect with them eye-to-eye...and most would smile back- a welcome connection to their part of humanity. Others would stare blankly at my smiling face, and not sure how to process the exchange, they would look back down at the phone in hand and keep moving on. Later on, back in the parking lot, it was a similar vibe- people leaving at the end of a very long day; to hurry home in rush hour traffic, to eat dinner, watch a little TV and fall into bed. Only to wake up to do it all over again.

While this does sound like a dismal view of an average life, I can assure you that the magic is out there. It is there, in that office building, that the little things, the shy smile in the maintenance man who takes pride in cleaning the escalator railings, the jovial FedEx delivery person who loved to talk about last night's sports wins or losses, the office worker who has everyone sign the card for the birthday celebrant du jour.

So, what if our PURPOSE in life isn't to make grand discoveries, cure illness, invent a new gadget- although those things are wonderful and have certainly advanced our society- but maybe that isn't the divine plan for all of us?

What if our purpose is simply to help make a difference in other people's lives? When we see someone struggle, we offer a helping hand. Or suspending judgment of another's situation, because we truly do not know the depth of their story.

What if our true PURPOSE is to simply be happy, grateful and be at peace with ourselves?

Before you dismiss this as too simplistic or even "Pollyanna-ish," let me remind you of what Eckhard Tolle says:

"Your primary purpose is to be here fully, and to be total in whatever you do so that the preciousness of the present moment does not become reduced to a means to an end. And there you have your life purpose. That's the very foundation of your life."

~ Eckhart Tolle

Or, consider this beautiful passage by Martha Graham:

"There is a vitality, a life force, a quickening that is translated through you into action, and there is only one of you in all time, this expression is unique, and if you block it, it will never exist through any other medium; and be lost. The world will not have it. It is not your business to determine how good it is, not how it compares with others expression. It is your business to keep it yours clearly and directly, to keep the channel open. You do not even have to believe in yourself or your work. You have to keep open and aware directly to the urges that motivate you. Keep the channel open. No artist is pleased. There is no satisfaction whatever at any time. There is only a queer, divine dissatisfaction, a blessed unrest that keeps us marching and makes us more alive than the others."

~ Martha Graham

I believe that we were born into this time for a reason. In some ways, we are at the forefront in leading humanity into the next phase of evolution. Hard to believe when we're witnessing so much anguish, hopelessness, anxiety and disconnect.

Underneath it all, there is a glimmer of hope.

When you honor your authentic self,
the energy is sent out into the universe
in ever increasing ripples-
much needed waves of Universal energy
that impacts those around us.

A few years ago, I was asked to present a talk on how to live more "ON Purpose." Since I like to create a visual along with my talks to keep people engaged, I came up with this explainer. The handout was a much more simplified version than what you see below, but I've elaborated to give you a deeper perspective.

PURPOSE

✦ P- Power ✦

This is the first step to consciously create your life. Stand in your Power, Peaceful Presence- and be deliberate about your energy. I'm not talking about power over another, I'm talking about the power within. You are a being of energy and light. Whatever you want to create in your life must come from your deepest self. Take a moment and connect with your energy- in and around your body.

✦ U- Unlock ✦

How do you unlock and uncover your hidden gifts and talents? Simply by tuning into yourself and know what lifts your heart. Let go of your limiting beliefs and start playing. Make art, take voice lessons, start writing that book, create from your heart. The challenge is to ignore the critical voices and let joy in. That looks different for everyone and getting to know yourself at the deepest level is key. Know what fills your heart with joy.

✦ R- Release ✦

Begin to identify limiting beliefs by observing how you speak to yourself. Notice things you say (or think) like "I'm not good at math," or "I can never do anything right." Get really clear on identifying the inner critic or the negative voice and begin to tell a new story. Say things like, "I I'm having fun learning a new skill" or, "I used to be frustrated with myself but now, I'm more compassionate with myself." Identify the old "stories" you tell yourself and release and let go old/outdated ones. Self-Compassion is the new way of being.

✦ P- Peace ✦

Walk through your day with a purposeful, peaceful presence. This is more a way of Being, rather than a "doing." Begin each day with a mantra or affirmation like, *"Today, I walk with Power, Peace, Presence and Purpose."* Say it now and feel your energy shift.

✦ O- Organize ✦

Clearing out clutter; (inner and outer, including digital). Clutter is a symbol of unfinished business and energetically it drags us down. This stage is ongoing, because there are always more things to let go of. The more we pursue spiritual growth, the more we discover things that no longer serve us. This is a powerful time to finally let go and clear our energy.

✦ S- Surrender ✦

This is not the same as giving up. Surrender is about allowing things and people to be as they are. It is about Acceptance and being at peace with what is. It is from this point you can make the necessary changes. We are constantly bombarded by many little (insidious) messages about who we should be, what we should wear, and what we should look like. It's no wonder that many are walking around with a thin layer of uncertainty and feelings of inadequacy. Add a few dollops of anxiety, and there's your recipe for the general malaise that permeates our society. By surrendering, you are making peace with what is and not struggling against what you think things should be. When you surrender, you are making peace with what is and not struggling against what you think things should be. When you surrender you stop struggling against the tide and your body relaxes into the now. You are still "present" just not trying to control everything.

✦ E- Energy ✦

Since everything is energy, this is where it all comes together. You are now embodying the energy of walking with Power, Peace, Presence and Purpose. You hold yourself differently, you interact with people differently, you begin to see the world through different eyes. Calling in all of your energy into your center (your core) brings together the scattered parts of you. When you worry about the past or the future, there are little pieces of you that are elsewhere. **Where** are your thoughts? Take a moment and come into the present moment.

REMEMBER:

Your true PURPOSE is to simply be happy, grateful and be at peace with yourself.

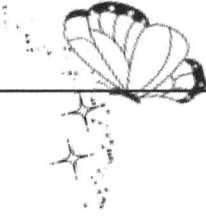

Chapter Summary:

Leading a Purpose Driven life is what many of us strive for- so we can leave our mark, make an impact and leave a legacy for the generations that come after or as Joe Dispenza says: "Purpose is what gives life meaning and direction. It's dynamic, uniquely personal, always evolving and never-ending."

Exercise:

Contemplate the Joe Dispenza quote above- then, write down the things that uplift you, speak to your heart and give you JOY.

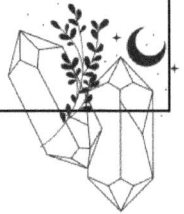

WHAT'S NEXT?

The purpose of this book has been to act as a guidepost to help you move along in your life with a new intention.

That intention is: living your life from a place of *Power, Peace, Presence and Purpose. To live a more soul aligned life.*

If you've stayed with me this far, I'm going to guess that you have a fair idea of how to proceed.

Although the concepts contained in this book are far from complicated, the real challenge lies in REMEMBERING. Make no mistake, living this way takes real focus and a mindset to become more of who we truly are.

If we are meant to make a difference and change the consciousness of humanity and move us closer to a more peaceful world, where there is cooperation and collaboration- it's going to take each and every one of us to make that commitment. And, who doesn't want to live a better, more peaceful and joyful life?

Once you finish this book, the next part is to start LIVING as a conscious being- taking an active role in creating a better life for yourself. I encourage you to start now (you don't need any fancy equipment) and keep this book handy. You can even pick it up in the morning and turn to a random page- let that be your focus for the day.

While thinking about how to wrap it up while giving a clear image for you on how to proceed. I decided to give you the task of being a visionary.

What is a visionary?

A visionary is someone who imagines a better self, a better community, a better future, a better world. Someone who can articulate that Vision to others so clearly- that its existence is felt merely by describing it.

The energy and emotion underneath the words paint the picture of this imagined future and is felt on a visceral level.

If you've ever heard someone describe their plans for something; something they've put their whole heart and soul into- you can feel the passion and get caught up and you begin to believe what's possible!!

It's absolutely electrifying and energizing and WE BELIEVE!

The true visionary isn't a self-serving vision; it comes from the deepest core; a universal truth and the greatest result is to the benefit of ALL. (Not just one or a few)

I believe we are all visionaries at heart.

We know there is so much more to our lives than we think. We all have within us a power that if we learn to harness, we can bring about the shift of the ages.

All we need to do is to make the decision to live more consciously.

Remember how I stated at the beginning of this book that we (most of us anyway) have forgotten that we are radiant, cosmic beings of energy?

Well, the time to remember that fact is NOW!

So go out, practice walking through life with *Power, Peace, Presence and Purpose!*

"When we make that decision to live more consciously, to set our intentions to live more fully to our purpose in life, it sets wheels in motion and will bring us opportunities that we could never dream of. We inspire others to live to their full potential and that ripples out into the world. We move beyond ourselves and our daily lives and that is how we impact humanity."

~ The BEGINNING

(FINAL THOUGHTS)

"If you feel lost, disappointed, hesitant, or weak, return to yourself, to who you are, here and now and when you get there, you will discover yourself, like a lotus flower in full bloom, even in a muddy pond, beautiful and strong."

~ Masaru Emoto - Secret Life of Water, 2004.

www.ingramcontent.com/pod-product-compliance
Lightning Source LLC
Chambersburg PA
CBHW071744020426
42331CB00008B/2163